THIS JOURNAL BELONGS TO:

____

PAPERLUSH

PRESS

PAPERLUSH

PRESS

Made in the USA
Coppell, TX
14 May 2021

55641486R10069